ACOUSTIC ROCK FOR GUITAR

By John Stix And Yoichi Arakawa

ISBN 0-7935-4375-4

HAL•LEONARD
CORPORATION

7777 W. BLUEMOUND RD. P.O. BOX 13819 MILWAUKEE, WI 53213

INTRODUCTION

In its short history, rock music has produced no band more melodically memorable than The Beatles or more raucous and bombastic than The Who. Coming from seemingly opposite directions, both bands lean on the acoustic guitar for the foundation of their songs. From Stone Temple Pilots to Led Zeppelin and Elvis Presley to Soul Asylum, the acoustic guitar has had a profound impact on the rock music that any generation calls their own. Media giant MTV has even made a side business out of bringing us the "Unplugged" sounds of electric artists from Nirvana to Eric Clapton.

The electricity of the acoustic guitar existed long before MTV discovered it. You can hear it used in: rock-influenced blues (Jimi Hendrix, "Hear My Train A Comin'," Eddie Van Halen, "Take Your Whiskey Home") folk music (Jimmy Page, "Black Mountain Side," The Allman Brothers, "Little Martha") classical music (Randy Rhoads "Dee," Yngwie Malmsteen, "Coming Bach") ethnic music (Robbie Krieger, "Spanish Caravan," Al DiMeola, "Mediterranean Sun-dance") and country music (Steve Howe, "Clap," George Harrison, "I've Just Seen A Face"). The acoustic guitar has also often been used as a songwriters tool. As it was true for rock composers in the '50s so it is four decades later. Kim Thayil of Soundgarden comments: "Most of our songs are written on bass, acoustic guitar, and frequently, a 12-string acoustic. Even our hardcore songs were written on acoustic guitar. It's just sped up and turned up when we put it on a record."

This *Pocket Guide To Acoustic Rock Guitar* will provide you with a user-friendly introduction to some classic strumming and fingerpicking techniques, using various rock songs for reference. Just spend as much time as you need with the Notation Legend, and let's play!

STRUMMING

Most people strum with a pick (Van Halen) or thumb pick (Johnny Winter), while some people use their thumb (Jeff Beck) or thumb and fingers (Steve Howe). There is no one right way to strum, just a variety of choices. Whether you choose to play with your fingers or with a pick is a personal decision based on the style of music and the sound you want to produce. Even Jimi Hendrix songs have been arranged for fingerstyle guitar!

NOTATION LEGEND

Down and Up Strokes:

This symbol (∏) indicates a downstroke (strumming toward the ground). This symbol (V) indicates an upstroke (strumming towards the ceiling).

Muting:

When playing open chords, mute or deaden the strings by lightly resting the palm of your strumming hand on the strings. When playing barre chords, you may use this same technique or simply lift your fretting hand slightly off the strings. Hall of Fame rhythm guitarists from Pete Townsend ("Won't Get Fooled Again") to Eddie Van Halen ("Little Guitars") use this technique to great advantage.

Accent:

This symbol (>) indicates an accent, which tells you to put more emphasis on a particular place in the music. Accents are a good way to spice up what you're playing.

Hammer-on:

Pick the first (lower) note, then "hammer-on" to sound the higher note with another finger by fretting it without picking.

Hammer-on

Pull-off:

Place both fingers on the notes to be sounded. Pick the first (higher) note, then sound lower note by "pulling-off" the finger on the higher note while keeping the lower note fretted.

Pull-off

Bending:

Pick the note and bend up.

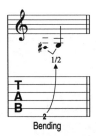

Bending

EXPLAINING TABLATURE

Tablature is a paint-by-number language telling you which notes to play on the fingerboard. Each of the six lines represents a string on the guitar. The numbers in the line indicate which frets to press down. Note that tablature does not indicate the rhythm.

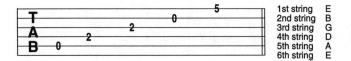

1st string	E
2nd string	B
3rd string	G
4th string	D
5th string	A
6th string	E

PRACTICE TIPS

1. Strive for a steady, fluid strum, alternating between downstrokes and upstrokes. Just as you do when with picking out riffs or solos, your controlled picking technique will define the "feel" of the music.

2. Keep your wrist loose.

3. Pay close attention to accents. They not only give you an edge and help define your style, but they also make strumming more percussive, particularly when combined with muting.

4. Downstrokes and upstrokes placed on the patterns are only suggestions by the authors. They are intended merely as a place to start. This is your music, so play the way you feel most comfortable or the way you want to hear it.

4

5. The best way to practice smooth and accurate strumming is to play with other musicians, or along with recorded music, a metronome, or a drum machine.

HOW TO READ RHYTHM CHARTS

The rhythm charts presented in the Strumming section observe the basic rules of music notation. The only difference is the use of slashes in place of conventional oval-shaped notes. Below is a brief review of various slash and rest symbols and an explanation of time signature. For greater details, please refer to music theory books.

Rhythm Slashes and Rests

Rhythm slashes tell you the duration of how long the chord being played should sound or sustain. For example, a whole note lasts for four counts or beats per measure, a quarter note for one count, and so on. Likewise, a rest tells you when to stop playing, and for how long. The following chart summarizes various note, slash and rest symbols. Counts or numbers of beats, indicate how many counts each chord should last (or be silent, in the case of rests) during a measure of 4/4.

NAME OF NOTE	NOTATION RHYTHM SLASH	REST SYMBOLS	COUNTS OR NUMBER OF BEATS
Whole Note	𝅝		1 2 3 4
Half Note	𝅗𝅥		1 2 3 4
Quarter Note	𝅘𝅥		1 2 3 4
Eighth Note	𝅘𝅥𝅮		1 & 2 & 3 & 4 &
Sixteenth Note	𝅘𝅥𝅯		1 2 3 4 2 2 3 4 3 2 3 4 4 2 3 4
Eighth-Note Triplet			1 2 3 2 2 3 3 2 3 4 2 3
*Dotted Quarter Note	𝅘𝅥.		1 & 2 3 & 4
*Dotted Eighth Note	𝅘𝅥𝅮.		1 2 3 4 2 2 3 4 3 2 3 4 4 2 3 4

*A dot increases a note value by one-half (eg: 𝅘𝅥. = 𝅘𝅥 + 𝅘𝅥𝅮 • 𝅗𝅥. = 𝅗𝅥 + 𝅘𝅥)

Time Signature

The time signature placed at the beginning of a piece of music tells you how to count time. It consists of two numbers, one placed above the other. The upper number tells you the number of beats in one measure. The lower number indicates what kind of note receives one beat, or count. For example, in 4/4, the most common and popular time signature, there are four beats to the measure, and a quarter note receives one beat. Below is a summary of various time signatures.

TIME SIGNATURES		EXAMPLES
$\frac{4}{4}$	4 beats per bar. A quarter note receives 1 beat.	♪ ♪ ♪ ♪ | ♩ ♪ ♪ 1 2 3 4 1 2 3 4
$\frac{2}{4}$	2 beats per bar. A quarter note receives 1 beat.	♪ ♪ | ♫ ♪ 1 2 1 & 2
$\frac{3}{4}$	3 beats per bar. A quarter note receives 1 beat.	♪ ♪ ♪ | ♪ ♫ ♫ 1 2 3 1 2 & 3 &
$\frac{6}{8}$	6 beats per bar. An eighth note receives 1 beat.	♫♫♫ ♫♫♫ | ♩ ♪♩ ♪ 1 2 3 4 5 6 1 2 3 4 5 6
$\frac{12}{8}$	12 beats per bar. An eighth note receives 1 beat.	♫♫♫♫♫♫♫♫ | ♩ ♪♩ ♪♩. ♩. 1 2 3 4 5 6 7 8 9 10 11 12 1 2 3 4 5 6 7 8 9 10 11 12

Tie

A tie is a curved line connecting two slashes of the same chord. It is an indication that the chord is to be sounded only once and held for the time value of both slashes combined.

	EXAMPLES		
1	♩‿♩	= ♩.	(3 beats)
2	♪‿ | ‿♪		(8 beats)
3	♪‿♪	= ♪.	(1 1/2 beats)
4	♪‿♪	= ♪	(1 beat)

All the songs on 'hints, allegations and things left unsaid' were started with an acoustic guitar.

—Ed Roland (Collective Soul)

BASIC STRUMMING EXAMPLES

The basic one-bar patterns listed in Exs. 1-75 are only a small portion of the endless possibilities available. Create your own by changing them or by using your imagination and starting from scratch. Remember, you can play any chord you like. For Exs. 1-15, we have given you simple patterns, using mainly quarter notes and eighth notes.

Ex. 1 is used in the Beatles song "Rocky Raccoon." See Ex. 92.

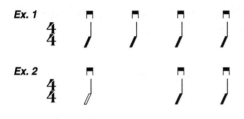

Ex. 3 can be used to play another Beatles classic, "Can't Buy Me Love." See Ex. 76. Reverse Ex. 3 and use all downstrokes to duplicate a strum from Led Zeppelin's "Babe I'm Gonna Leave You." See Ex. 80.

A variation of Ex. 4 can be heard in the opening bar of Rod Stewart's "Maggie May." See Ex. 77.

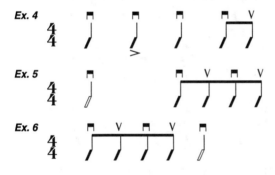

Ex. 7 will get you started playing Guns N' Roses' "Used to Love Her." See Ex. 82.

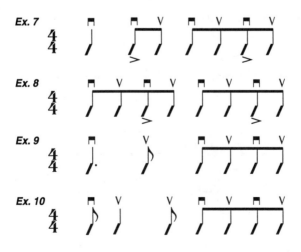

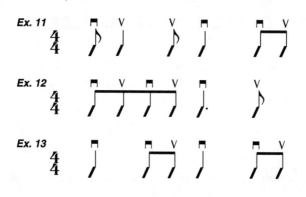

Ex. 14 is used by The Allman Brothers Band in the song "Jessica." See Ex. 93.

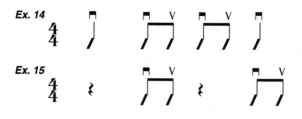

Exs. 16-21 show off various syncopation patterns. With ties, the accents fall onto the normally weak or unaccented beats (usually upbeats).

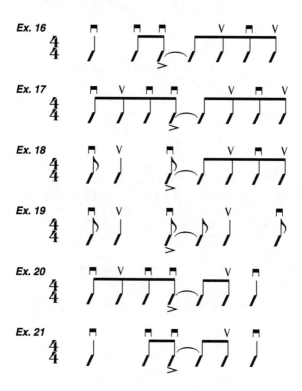

Exs. 22-31 provide you with examples to practice muting.

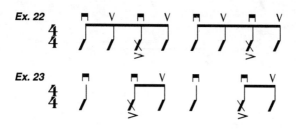

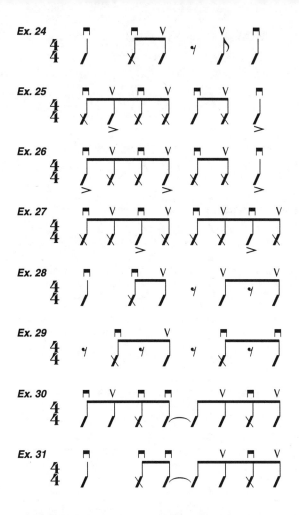

Exs. 32-52 introduce the sixteenth note. Ex. 32 is used to play the outro of James Taylor's "Fire and Rain." See Ex. 99.

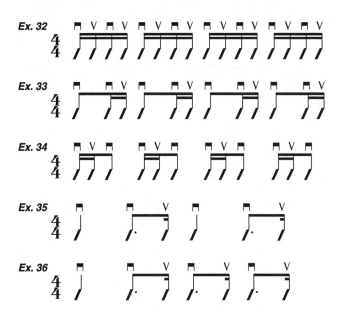

Ex. 37 is used to play "Pinball Wizard" by The Who. See Ex. 97.

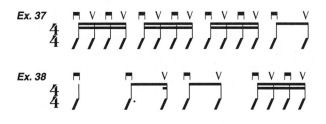

Ex. 39 is similar to Mr. Big's "To Be With You." See Ex. 98.

I started as an acoustic player because I felt Buddy Holly used
that a lot. It was his principle sound. The Beatles used that as a
presence as well. A very strong acoustric guitar. When I was a
kid, my first guitar was an acoustic.

—Justin Hayward (The Moody Blues)

Exs. 53-64 are examples in 3/4. This means there are 3 beats (instead of 4) in a measure and the quarter note gets one beat. Ex. 53 is used to play "How Will I Ever Be Simple Again" by Richard Thompson. See Ex. 94.

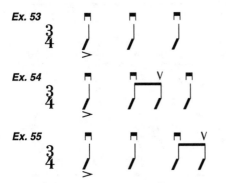

A variation of Ex. 56 is used by Steve Howe in Yes' "Mood For A Day." See Ex. 81.

Ex. 56

Ex. 57 will get you started on The Eagles' "Hollywood Waltz." See Ex. 86.

A variation of Ex. 58 is used by The Eagles on "Take It To the Limit."

Exs. 66-75 explore shuffle patterns in 12/8. There are 12 beats in each measure and the eighth notes gets one beat. Remember that each group of 3 beats has a triplet feel.

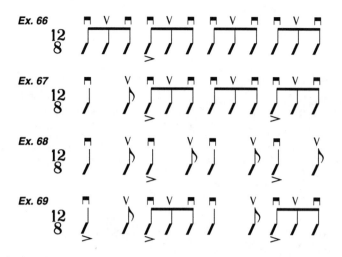

Ex. 66

Ex. 67

Ex. 68

Ex. 69

Ex. 70 will get you started on The Eagles' "Journey of the Sorcerer." See Ex. 91. Another variation of Ex. 70 is used by Eric Clapton on "Alberta." See Ex. 92.

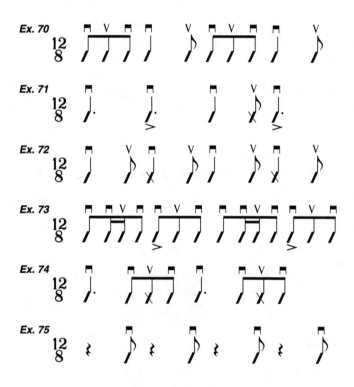

Ex. 70

Ex. 71

Ex. 72

Ex. 73

Ex. 74

Ex. 75

SONG EXAMPLES

The following are examples inspired by famous songs that feature the acoustic guitar. You'll notice that all kinds of groups and singer/songwriters have used the acoustic guitar to create legendary parts that are as indelible as any to come from a Marshall stack and a Stratocaster.

Ex. 76 is the rhythm pattern you'd use to play The Beatles' "Can't Buy Me Love."

Ex. 76

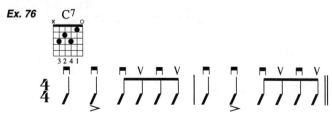

C⁷

Ex. 77 is very similar to what you'd play on Rod Stewart's "Maggie May."

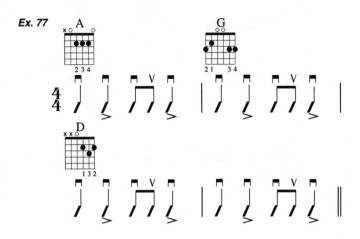

Ex. 78 sounds much like the hook in Tom Petty's "Free Fallin'."

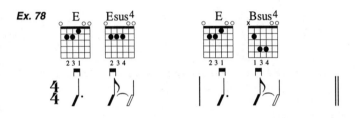

Ex. 79 will get you close to Nirvana's "Come As You Are."

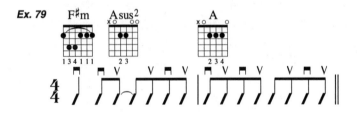

Ex. 80 echoes part of Led Zeppelin's "Babe I'm Gonna Leave You."

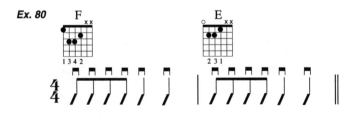

Ex. 81 reminds us of the opening to "Mood for a Day" by Yes.

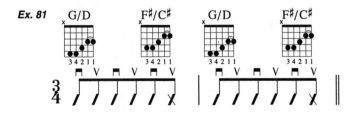

Ex. 82 is the rhythm pattern used to play "Used to Love Her" by Guns N' Roses.

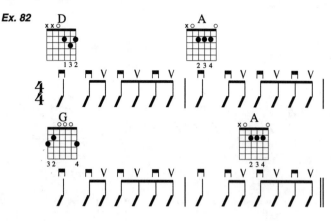

Ex. 83 is very similar to what Stephen Stills plays on "Make Love to You."

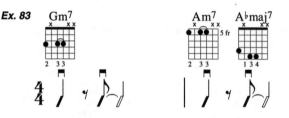

Ex. 84 sounds much like another section from "Babe I'm Gonna Leave You" by Led Zeppelin.

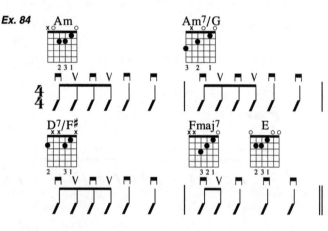

Ex. 85 may remind you of a part in "Hollywood Waltz" by The Eagles.

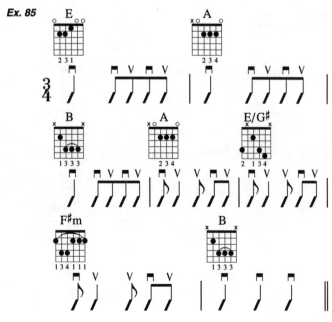

Ex. 86 was inspired by The Eagles' "Lying Eyes."

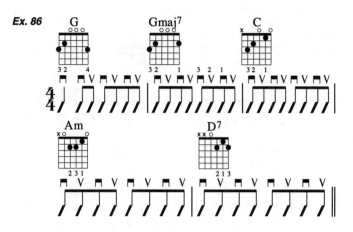

Ex. 87 echoes in the style of The Eagles' "Take It Easy."

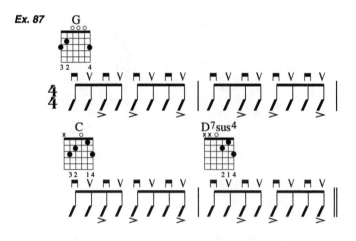

Ex. 88: The Eagles' "New Kid in Town" was the inspiration for these rhythm patterns.

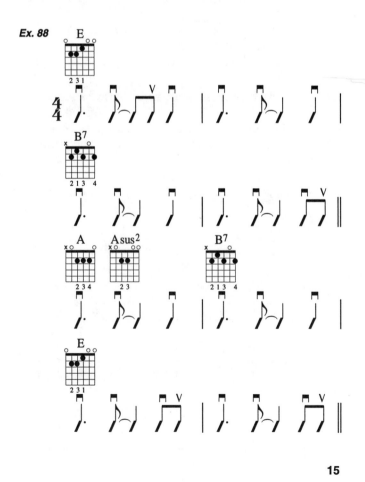

Ex. 89 reminds us of what Eric Clapton played on "San Francisco Bay Blues."

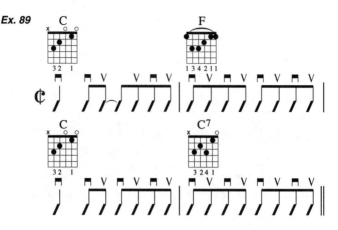

Ex. 90 was inspired by the Eagles' "Journey Of The Sorcerer."

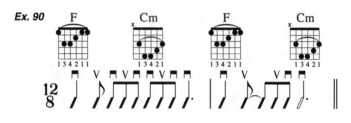

Ex. 91 has its roots in "Alberta" by Eric Clapton.

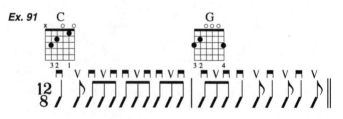

People have told us over and over again that the acoustic songs are their favorite part of the show.
—David Crosby (Crosby, Stills, and Nash)

Exs. 92-96 use the Carter Family style, which consists of alternating bass notes with chords. It can be played using a flat-pick, or by letting the thumb pick out the bass notes, while the index and middle fingers of the right-hand strum the higher strings.

Ex. 92 is reminiscent of "Rocky Raccoon" by The Beatles.

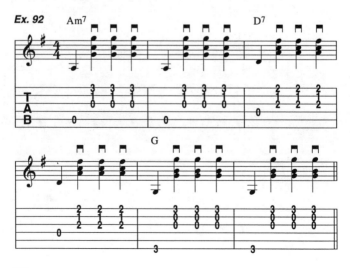

Ex. 93 is in the style of the opening chords from "Jessica" by The Allman Brothers Band.

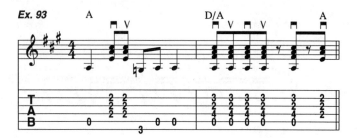

Ex. 94 is in the style of Richard Thompson's "How Will I Ever Be Simple Again."

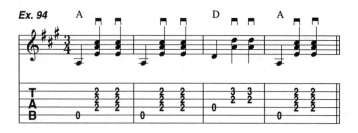

Ex. 95 has its roots in the Crosby, Stills and Nash classic, "Helplessly Hoping."

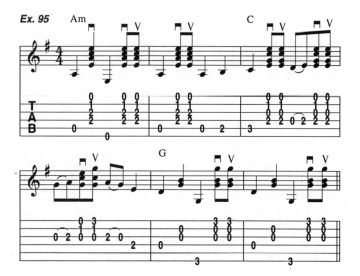

Ex. 96 is inspired by Emerson, Lake and Palmer's "From The Beginning."

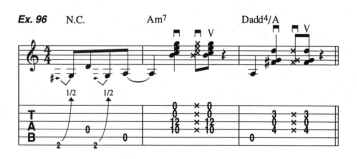

Ex. 97 became a classic move in The Who's "Pinball Wizard." To get it just right, you must play it smoothly.

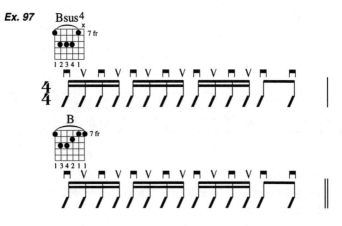

Ex. 98 was used in Mr. Big's "To Be With You."

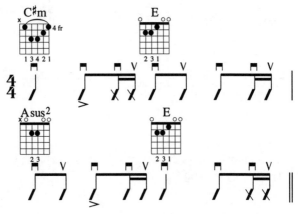

Ex. 99 was inspired by the outro to James Taylor's "Fire and Rain." Notice how changing one note from A9 (no 3rd) to Asus2 can have a dramatic effect on the music.

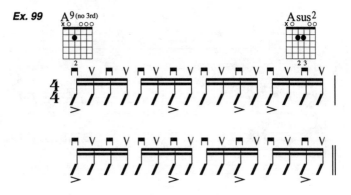

Ex. 100 is an idea we heard in Eric Clapton's "Running on Faith." Notice the progression of the second to third chords, where the inner voice is the only movement.

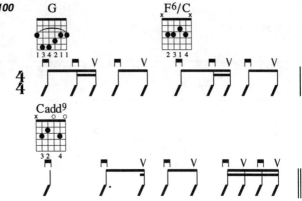

Ex. 101 has its roots in Pink Floyd's "Wish You Were Here." Notice how the first chord has the 5th in the bass note, and the second has its 3rd in the bass note, creating a smooth descending bass line.

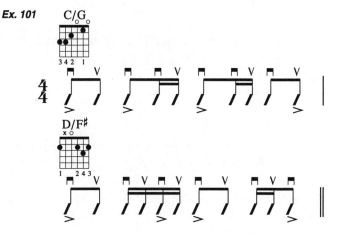

Ex. 102 was like something we heard in Sheryl Crow's "Leaving Las Vegas." The move from Dsus4 to D is one of the most popular chord changes in rock songwriting.

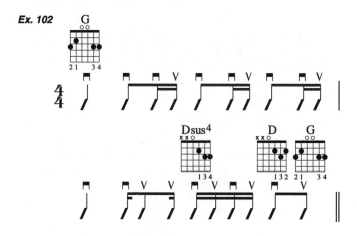

Ex. 103 was inspired by Jethro Tull's "Cheap Day Return." To play along with the record, you will need to use a capo on the 7th fret.

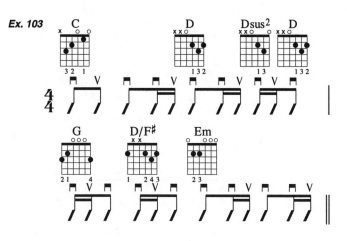

Ex. 104 comes by way of Jethro Tull's "Up to Me." It's a nice open-chord progression.

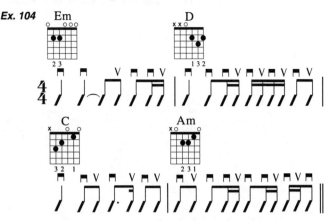

Ex. 105 has its roots in "Tangerine" by Led Zeppelin. Notice the descending bass line from one chord to another, which requires quite a stretch.

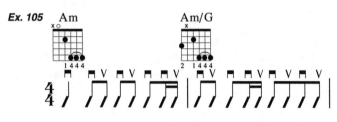

Ex. 106 was something we heard in "Gallows Pole," from Led Zeppelin, which shows movement from a major to a minor chord. This was done by changing the C# to C.

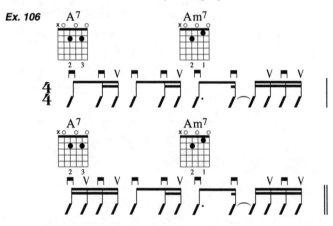

Ex. 107 is similar to a part from the Led Zeppelin classic, "Your Time is Gonna Come."

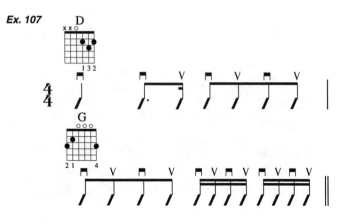

The song that gives me a kick from 'Appetite' is 'Brownstone.' It was written on acoustic guitar.

—Izzy Stradlin (Guns N' Roses)*

*Courtesy of *Guitar for the Practicing Musician Magazine*

FINGERSTYLE

Fingerstyle is a popular and useful technique often used by "singer/songwriter"- type performers for playing accompaniment to their singing, or for solo guitar pieces. Most fingerstyles widely used today are a product of classical and traditional folk techniques. This combination of the studied (classical) and the unschooled (folk/blues) shows you the flexibility of this style of guitar playing. That is, learn what you can, and apply it to your own music with an "anything goes" approach.

RIGHT-HAND POSITION

One way to approach the picking-hand position is to pretend that your right hand (picking hand) is lightly gripping the right handlebar of a motorcycle. Now bring your arm down so your hand is lightly touching the strings. You've got your thumb out in front of your fingers and pointed toward the neck. Your other fingers are loosely curled, and by moving your hand to a slight angle they will naturally fall into a position where the index, middle, and ring fingers each have their own string to pluck. The important thing is to play with a relaxed picking hand. So experiment until you find the position that is most comfortable for you.

Although the choice of fingering is a personal matter, we'll start with the most common fingering. The thumb will hit the bass strings (E, A, D) with a downstroke. While using upstrokes, the index finger (i) plays the G, the middle finger (m) plays the B, and the ring finger (a) plays the high E string.

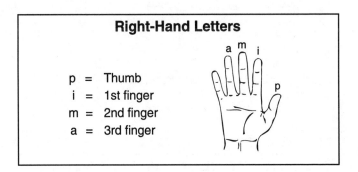

Right-Hand Letters

p = Thumb
i = 1st finger
m = 2nd finger
a = 3rd finger

BASIC STYLES

The following style explanation and 1-bar examples will give you an idea of how fingerpicking works. It will also help you to develop independent finger control, which is essential for this style. This foundation should make it easier to play and understand the examples we've chosen. They are all inspired from various fingerstyle songs, which in turn should be a starting point for discovering your own patterns.

Arpeggios

Arpeggios are played by holding a chord and playing one note after another in sequence, each note sounding separately.

Exs. 108 and 109 are basic arpeggio patterns. In Ex. 108, the high G and B notes are plucked simultaneously, so become one sound. In Ex. 109, we suggest you play the first two notes with your thumb.

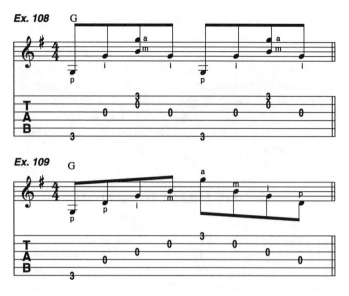

Travis Picking (Double Thumbing)

Travis picking is a technique where your thumb plays every other note. This develops a bass line on the lower strings while a melody is played on the higher strings. See Exs. 110 and 111.

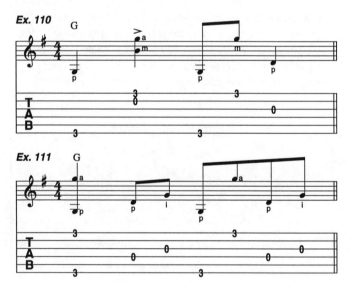

Pick and Fingers

One of the more versatile approaches to acoustic or electric playing is to use a combination of the pick and your fingers. Even guitarists from Eddie Van Halen to Albert Lee have put in some time with this one. Go slow and have your pick do the downstrokes while your fingers do the upstrokes. See Exs. 112 and 113.

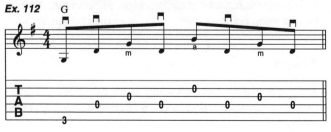

Ex. 113

Flatpicking

In place of your fingers, you can use a pick to arpeggiate chords. Bands like Candlebox, The Black Crowes, and Gin Blossoms have used this style to good effect. Al DiMeola learned to flatpick so fast because he was trying to imitate Doc Watson, but what he didn't know was that Doc was fingerpicking his parts. At the end of the day, Al learned to duplicate Doc's flatpicking with just a pick, and developed his own style in the process! Using that as our model, try to play all of the following examples with a pick, or any style you like. See Exs. 114 and 115.

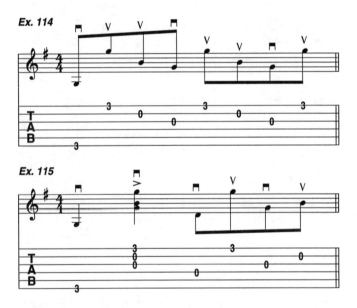

Ex. 114

Ex. 115

PRACTICE TIPS

1. As with strumming, it is very important to keep a smooth, steady rhythm. Playing along with a drum machine should help your timing.

2. For all of the examples, hold each chord while you are picking and let each note ring.

3. Experiment with different fingers or different picking styles. If something works better for you because it feels right, then it *is* right!

I don't play a lot of electric at home. I tend to play acoustic because it is my main direction.

—Steve Howe (Yes)

SONG EXAMPLES

The following are song examples that use the fingerpicking style:

Ex. 116 is the Travis-style pattern that Paul Simon used in "American Tune."

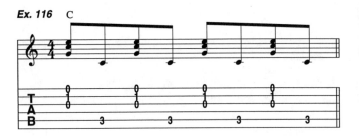

Ex. 117 is a fingerpicking pattern similar to Led Zeppelin's "Babe I'm Gonna Leave You."

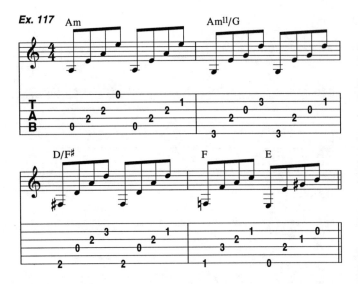

Ex. 118 is inspired by Greg Lake's fingerpicking in Emerson, Lake and Palmer's "From the Beginning."

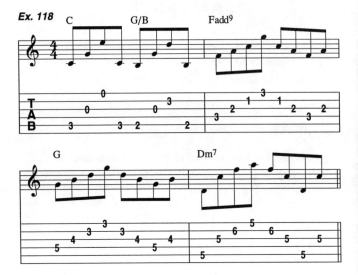

Ex. 119 has its roots in Led Zeppelin's classic, "Stairway to Heaven."

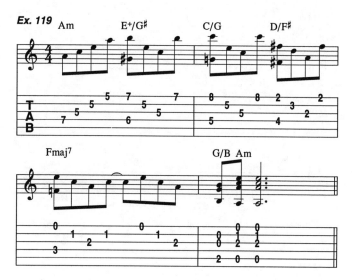

Ex. 120 is similar to Jim Croce's intro to "I'll Have to Say I Love You in a Song."

Ex. 121 was inspired by Jim Croce's "Operator."

Ex. 122 has its roots in the song "If" by Bread.

Ex. 122

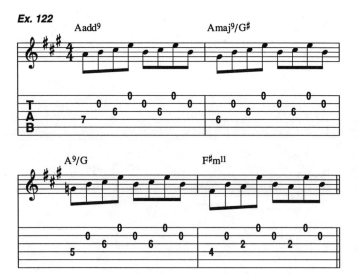

Ex. 123 is a lot like James Taylor's rendition of "You've Got a Friend."

Ex. 123

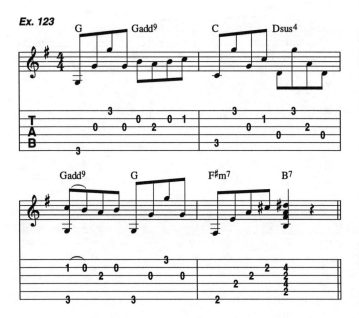

Ex. 124 resembles an Al DiMeola line from "Electric Rendezvous."

Ex. 124

Ex. 125 was inspired by Extreme's hit, "More Than Words."

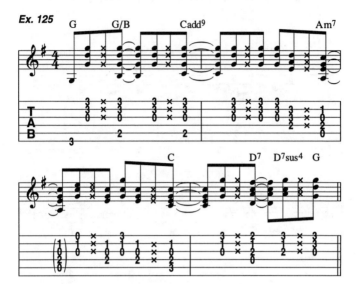

Ex. 126 echoes the opening chords of "Helplessly Hoping" from Crosby, Stills and Nash.

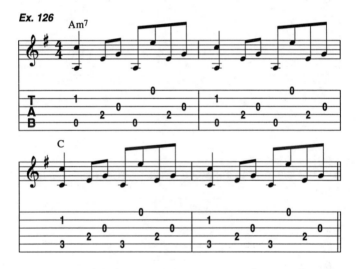

Ex. 127 was inspired by "Dust in the Wind" by Kansas. This is a good place to begin to explore your Travis picking. Over the next few examples, you'll find various illustrations of this technique.

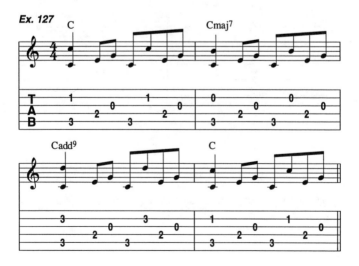

Ex. 128 is another example of Travis picking, this time reflecting the Blind Faith tune, "Can't Find My Way Home."

Ex. 128

Ex. 129 is similar to the Steven Stills bit in "Haven't We Lost Enough."

Ex. 129

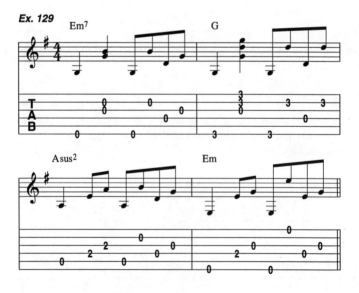

'Call Me the Breeze' and 'Cocaine' I wrote on an old $50 Harmony acoustic guitar.

—*J.J. Cale**

Ex. 130 is a take on another Stephen Stills tune, "Thorough-fare Gap."

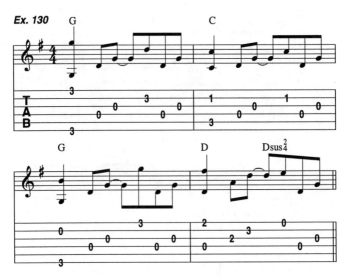

Ex. 131 was inspired by Jethro Tull's "Sossity You're A Woman."

Ex. 132 may remind you of Eric Clapton's "Tears in Heaven."

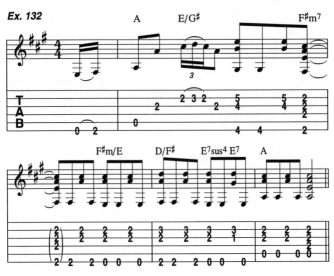

Ex. 133 resembles "Blackbird" by The Beatles.

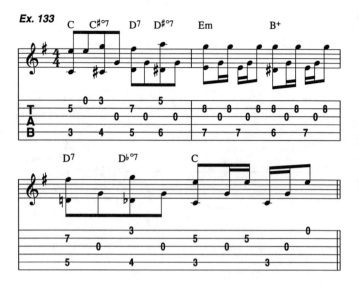

Ex. 134 is similar to "Send Me An Angel" by Scorpions.

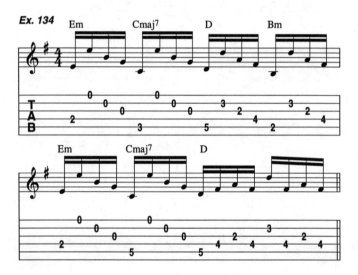

Ex. 135 was inspired by Bon Jovi's "Wanted Dead or Alive."

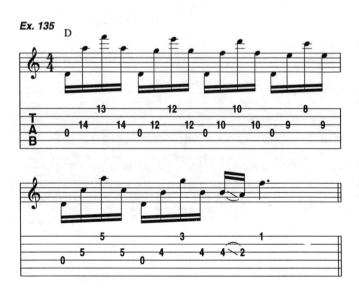

Ex. 136 is a take on Led Zeppelin's "Your Time Is Gonna Come."

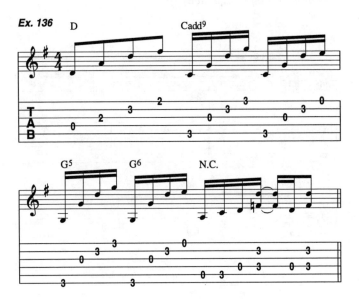

Ex. 137 is similar to Sheryl Crow's "Strong Enough."

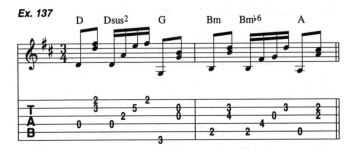

Ex. 138 resembles a line from "Passion, Grace and Fire" by John McLaughlin, Al DiMeola and Paco DeLucia.

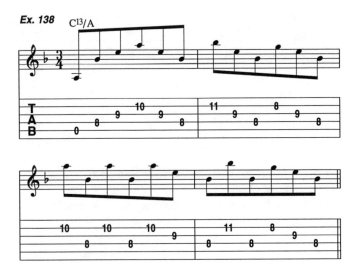

Ex. 139 was inspired by Jim Croce's "Time in a Bottle." It's a classic arpeggio figure with the bass line descending in half steps (one fret at a time).

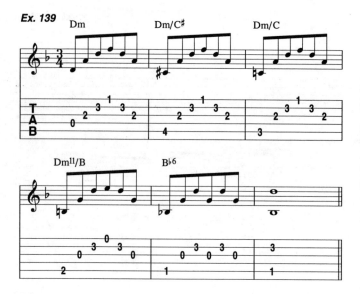

Ex. 140 is a bit of "Fluff," from Black Sabbath.

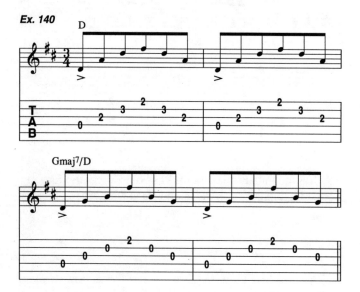

Since the first song I've written, it has always been done on an acoustic guitar. On the acoustic guitar, I'm more inclined to be looking for a melody within the chord structure. From a songwriter's point of view, when I sit down with an acoustic, I'm thinking melody—I'm thinking of hooks.

—Jon Bon Jovi (Bon Jovi)*